TERENCE CUNEO

RAILWAY PAINTER OF THE CENTURY

NARISA CHAKRA

New Cavendish Books

For Hugo

First edition published in Great Britain by New Cavendish Books – 1990

Design – John B Cooper
Production and supervision – Narisa Chakra
Editorial direction – Allen Levy

Copyright © collective work – New Cavendish Books – 1989
Copyright © paintings and sketches – Terence Cuneo – 1989
Typesetting & mono illustrations, Wyvern Typesetting Ltd, Bristol.
Printed and bound in Hong Kong under the supervision of Mandarin Offset
London.
New Cavendish Books, 3 Denbigh Road, London W11 2SJ
ISBN 0 904568 74 1

A history of the railway paintings of Terence Cuneo is also a chronicle of British Rail itself.

Over the years he has faithfully recorded the development of our railway network during a period of exceptional change. His brush has painstakingly depicted the last years of the steam era and the dramatic impact of diesel and electric traction during the first great modernization plan. Recently he has continued the story, painting the new 140 mph Class 91 electric locomotives which will take BR into the 1990s.

His accuracy of observation is legendary. So too is his determination to capture a subject in its natural surroundings, however precarious or uncomfortable a position that means. The results of such dedication are always outstanding.

Terence Cuneo's paintings have rarely been an end in themselves. Many have provided the raw material for posters which have delighted generations of our customers while keeping them informed of our progress; posters which themselves are now avidly sought after by collectors.

This book will give much happiness to Terence Cuneo's many admirers. And I am sure it too will become a collector's item.

Contents

Terence Cuneo at his easel painting 'Voice of the Giant',
German State Railways c. 1978

Introduction

In June 1988, a major retrospective was held at the Mall Galleries to celebrate Terence Cuneo's 80th birthday. Opened by H.R.H. The Duke of Edinburgh, it featured some 305 paintings covering all aspects of Cuneo's wide-ranging *oeuvre* of the last forty years. Such major works as 'The Coronation' or State Occasions and battle scenes, together with more personal paintings were all included, but undoubtedly one of the most popular sections was 'Cuneo Junction' containing 50 of the artist's best railway paintings. At times that room was packed to overflowing and some visitors reportedly lingered for hours, poring over every detail of their favourite trains.

Ever since its inception in the early years of the nineteenth century, the railways and their main actors, the locomotives, have been a potent inspiration for artists and engravers; at first for their topicality as seen in the many nineteenth century prints; later for their social content in such famous works as Frith's 'Railway Station' of 1862, or for their atmospheric and compositional possibilities as seen in Turner's 'Rain, Steam and Speed' and Monet's 'Gare St. Lazare'. In this century such artists as the futurist Gino Severini have used the train to symbolize the movement and dislocation of modern life; while de Chirico or Magritte have concentrated on the purely symbolic power of the train as an image.

After the 1960s with the demise of steam and the arrival of diesel, not only have the trains themselves become less romantic and evocative, but also avant-garde artists have turned to other concerns. However, the end of steam has not been accompanied by a lessening of its appeal for the public – perhaps even the reverse

and thus the role of artists like Terence Cuneo or David Shepherd has become even more important. It is through the depiction by Terence Cuneo of steam locomotives from all over the world that these magnificent machines can live again.

Terence Cuneo was born in London on November 1, 1907, the only son of Cyrus and Nell Cuneo. Cyrus was a talented Italian-American illustrator and onetime flyweight boxing champion of San Francisco, while Nell was formerly Nell Tenison, a cousin of the Poet Laureate. The two had met in Paris where Cyrus was training under Whistler. He was to become an extremely successful illustrator working mainly for *The*

Terence Cuneo with the Shepherds.

The infant Terence with his mother, painted by Cyrus Cuneo, 1908.

Illustrated London News. Although rather distant as was the custom in those days, he nevertheless indulged his young son with the gift of a toy engine thus encouraging what was to be a lifelong love affair with locomotives. Sadly, Cyrus Cuneo died in 1916 of blood poisoning and thereafter Terence's early artistic education was left in the hands of his mother. She had also trained in Paris and was herself very talented, although latterly she had assisted her husband rather than concentrating on her own work.

Terence Cuneo's early drawings have fortunately been preserved and already his interest in railway engines is clear. With friends he would invent elaborate stories, suitably illustrated, and a mythical railway company was formed staffed mainly by teddy bears and other animals. Meanwhile Cuneo's formal education was somewhat erratic as his mother, depressed after her husband's death, made several moves settling eventually in Cornwall at St. Ives. Later, journeys to and from school in Kent gave Cuneo an opportunity to study Brunel's Great Western Railway, in particular his magnificent Saltash Bridge and the beautiful coastal stretch between Dawlish and Teignmouth. As the 'King' or 'Castle' burst from the tunnel, Cuneo's eyes would eagerly seek out the curiously shaped red rock which signified the end of school and the beginning of the holidays. St. Ives at that time was a wonderful place for a nascent artist as there was a thriving artist's colony. Cuneo mother and son centred their lives around the Arts Club. His urge to draw and paint was becoming ever stronger and it was here that Cuneo made his first experiments in oils under the guidance of his mother.

Leaving school at seventeen there was no doubt in Cuneo's mind that like his father he would become an

AN. INDIAN. TRAIN

AN. AMERICAN. TRAIN.

A. RUSSAIN. TRAIN.

AN. AFRICAN. TRAIN

GREAT. WESTERN. RAILWAY.

artist and he enrolled at the Chelsea Polytechnic. By all reports, he did not enjoy a particularly distinguished career as an art student. Indeed, Cuneo was more interested in pursuing girls than attending his life classes. Some twenty years later, his one-time principal, Peter Jowett, met Cuneo's wife in front of a large painting of Lloyds underwriters exhibited in the Royal Academy and upon being told that it was by his erstwhile pupil exclaimed 'Terence *Cuneo* did *that*? I don't believe it; I simply cannot believe it! Why he was one of the most unpromising students I ever had.'

Nevertheless after completing his time at Chelsea Poly and with much touting around of his portfolio, Cuneo aged 19 began to bring in a modest amount of work as an illustrator of boy's magazines. Mention of his father's name often opened the door and although, at first, his work was compared unfavourably, soon commissions were coming in on a regular basis.

It was in the mid-1920s whilst living in Bedford Park that Cuneo had his first experience of driving a steam engine – a never-to-be-forgotten day. Soon he became proficient in shunting and the practical knowledge gained on the branch line was to be invaluable in his later portrayal of locomotives on canvas. It was by driving such monsters that he gained a knowledge of the strength and weight of a locomotive, feelings that must be conveyed by a successful railway painter.

Throughout the early 1930s, Cuneo's career as an illustrator gradually prospered, although money and deadlines were a constant problem, especially after September 1934 when he married Catherine Monro. It was at this period that Cuneo turned to writing stories as well as illustrating them in order to augment his

meagre income. The stories of necessity had a dramatic flavour and if possible Cuneo would include or base the story around some event on the railways. A typical example was his 1939 story for the *Champion Annual for Boys*, 'Cash on Delivery', in which two boys venture into a tunnel, and stumbling on a crime eventually catch the villain and receive a reward. Stirring stuff, and Cuneo's descriptions of the mighty engines thundering by prefigure his future experiences while working on the poster 'On Early Shift' at Greenwood Signal Box (see page 35). It shows that in words as well as paint, he could evocatively convey the power of steam:

''On she came, her massive boiler front towering gigantic above them, her funnel sending cannon-like smoke clouds up to the tunnel roof, her safety valve spurting a geyser of orange-lit steam into the swirling fumes above . . . They saw a sweating fireman pitch coal through the fire hold, and feasted their eyes on the elaborate array of twisting pipes and gauges and wheels on the boiler head!''

The accompanying drawings, executed in a powerful black and white style reminiscent of woodcuts, while not in themselves very remarkable, are significant in

11

France, 1940.
Illustrated London News.

Weights
CIGARETTES

a Player product - ever popular

that they represent his first commercial railway illustrations.

Gradually, Cuneo was able to improve the quality of his commissions, deserting the boys' annuals for such publications as *Strand Magazine*, *The London* and *Good Housekeeping*. He also worked much more in oils. However, the outbreak of war was soon to change the direction of Cuneo's career and he found himself working almost exclusively on war illustration for *The Illustrated London News*, *War Illustrated* and *Picture Post*. In 1940, a trip to France to tour armaments factories led, aside from his commissioned work, to a rare opportunity to ride a French train and make an excellent drawing of its fireman.

In November 1941, Cuneo's artistic work was cut short, when he was called up to join the Royal Corps of Signals. Not cut out to be a soldier, Cuneo did not enjoy this period of his life until the Ministry of Information commissioned him to do paintings of the resistance workers in France. One thing led to another and soon Cuneo was working on drawings of Nazi atrocities, plans of harbours and later work on the Mulberry harbour used for the D Day invasion. The experience provided by these commissions was invaluable, enabling Cuneo to turn his hand to a great variety of subjects and to work at speed with accuracy.

Another seemingly insignificant commission came his way during this period – that of a small book entitled *How to draw Tanks*. A letter from a Mr. George Garland requesting further information on tank drawing was to lead to a meeting which in turn led to Cuneo joining the War Artists Advisory committee under Sir Kenneth Clark. More commissions followed which indirectly were to lead in 1946 to Cuneo's first important railway commission – a poster for the LNER entitled 'Giants Refreshed'. Another for the LMS quickly followed and from then there was to be no looking back. Commissions came in thick and fast and have continued to do so ever since.

At eighty, Terence Cuneo is as lively as ever, a charming man with a trim figure and a twinkle in his eye; easy to talk to and very down to earth, despite having painted the Queen several times and many grand occasions. He still paints virtually every day and is as enthusiastic as many a man half his age.

'The Railway Station' by Frith.

During the course of several interviews, Cuneo also talked about his painting methods, which could be observed in the various stages in the completion of the painting of the new Class 91 for British Rail.

Throughout his life, Cuneo has kept a large scrapbook on trains, and ideas inspired by this, his numerous and carefully kept sketchbooks, a recent trip abroad or a specific commission may all serve as the trigger for a new composition. A small painting might take some three or four days to complete, whereas a more complicated commission such as the APT might require extensive preliminary work and study. Ideally, preliminary sketches will be done from the actual locomotive, but where this is not possible, a trip to the Science Museum, the London Toy and Model Museum, or the loan of a model locomotive from a friend must suffice. Where a commission calls for an unusual or exacting perspective, careful drawings are

'Rain Steam & Speed' by Turner.

'Gare St. Lazare' by Monet.

also made on the location, and, on occasion this has led to some hair-raising experiences whether in dark tunnels or many feet up on various railway bridges.

When painting begins, Terence Cuneo will often place a canvas on the floor to block in the basic colour areas, colour notes having been recorded on his preparatory sketches. Then the canvas is placed on the easel and work continues. The colour balance is worked up and gradually more detail is added as the locomotive takes life. Like most artists, Cuneo is reluctant to allow outsiders to see unfinished works, but occasionally, as in the case with some British Rail commissions, an expert on the particular locomotives might be called in

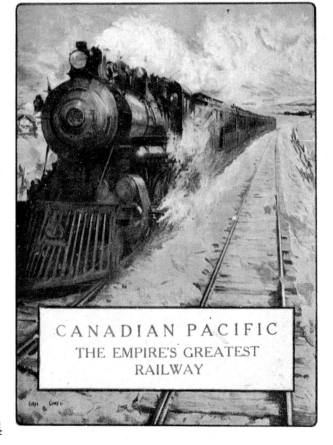

An illustration for the Canadian Pacific Railway by the artist's father, Cyrus Cuneo.

14

to give any advice needed. If a painting is not going well, Cuneo will continue to 'have a go at it' and admits to never giving up. It is this very tenacity which is an important quality of the man and his work, not only enabling him to work in all kinds of conditions, but also giving him tremendous drive and vitality.

In talking about the artists he admired, Cuneo demonstrated a very Catholic taste, although it would be true to say that he has never appreciated the more avant garde artists of his day. Just after the war, incensed by a Picasso exhibition at the Victoria and Albert Museum, he made a brief foray into the world of non-figurative painting, but has stated that it was his first and last attempt. Similarly, looking at nineteenth century artists and their portrayal of the railway engine, it is Frith whom Cuneo admires rather than Turner, declaring that the latter's 'Rain, Steam and Speed' ("You can hardly see the engine!") has always annoyed him intensely. Conversely, Cuneo is full of praise for Constable and his portrayal of the English countryside. Cuneo regrets that, unlike his father, he never had the chance of studying in Paris and not surprisingly he has always admired Monet's Gare St. Lazare series.

In this century there is little doubt that the work of his father, Cyrus Cuneo, has been of the greatest influence, although the son recently remarked with a smile on looking at his father's representation of a Canadian Pacific locomotive that "he's got the angle all wrong and the cow-catcher is far too big!" Other artists admired by Cuneo are Frank Brangwyn and Paul Nash.

Influences aside, the clue to appreciating Cuneo's work is probably his statement that he "doesn't paint to please anybody" – anybody that is but himself and he insists that he remains his own most rigorous critic. Integrity to his work and subject matter is paramount and often this has led to much discomfort and even danger, such as painting in a 53 mph gale on the Forth Bridge or dodging express trains at night outside Euston station. Confident in his work, Cuneo has little time for art critics, feeling that in many instances they may do more harm than good. Secure in the very English tradition of figurative painting, one might almost say a latter-day Alfred Munnings, Terence Cuneo has created his own role and in the genre of railway painting can certainly be acclaimed as 'The Railway Painter of the Century'.

Sketching on the tender of 'The Great Marquess' outside Birmingham.

← Terence Cuneo working on his largest ever commission (10 feet × 20 feet), showing the concourse of Waterloo Station in 1967. The painting is housed in the railway section of the Science Museum.

Terence Cuneo has always seized any and every opportunity of driving a steam locomotive. These photographs show some of the diverse engines he has driven:

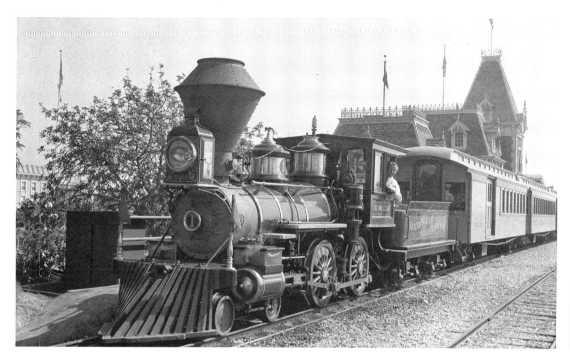

Disneyland. Driving with the special permission of Walt Disney 1956.

On an old 'Mogul' in Canada.

Here is the engine offered to Cuneo by the Managing Director of Newton Chambers. Unfortunately, Cuneo did not realize he was serious and has regretted ever since not accepting the engine.

Riding the cab of the 'Canadian' before leaving for the Rockies.

The Posters

In his autobiography, *The Mouse and his Master* Cuneo describes the period in which he first started work on his commissions for railway posters as "one of the happiest periods of my working life". Towards the end of the war, Cuneo accepted a series of aircraft commissions of many of the famous Second World War aircraft including the Mosquito, Hurricane, Spitfire, Lancaster and the Wellington – and he has stated that it was these paintings seen by the publicity manager of the LNER which led to his first commission for a painting which would be made into a railway poster. Elsewhere, he claimed that it was the painting executed in 1942 of an Essex water mill and exhibited at the London Sketch Club annual exhibition some years later which led the

same man to request a copy for use as a poster and thereafter further commissions. Whatever the truth of the matter there is little doubt that the series of paintings done for British Rail, and made into Quad Royal Posters, over the next forty years are among his finest work.

Tremendous trouble was taken by the artist to achieve an accurate and satisfying result – if the paintings seem so effortless that they led one observer to remark "It must be lovely sitting there in your cosy studio painting all those pictures", it is purely due to his skill as an artist. In addition, Cuneo has said that he was tremendously helped by all the railway officials involved who were always intensely enthusiastic and cooperative.

Giants Refreshed – 1946, 38" x 48" (poster 40" x 50")

This was Terence Cuneo's first commission for British Rail and it shows an A4 and an A2 LNER locomotive being painted in Doncaster Shed. Whilst Cuneo may be best remembered for his action paintings in which the locomotives seem ready to plunge off the canvas, in more static paintings such as this, his use of well-observed detail, such as the foreground scene of the man and his multi-coloured pots of paint, helps to give the painting its interest and vitality. This painting was to be the first of a whole series of station shed interiors painted throughout his forty year career, in which architectural elements and contrasting diagonals and verticals are combined to give the painting a firm structure.

It also shows Cuneo's light touch and use of the odd dog or cat to enliven a painting. This railway cat, who seemed to produce innumerable kittens, was included in the preparatory sketches and finally moved to a frontal position staring fixedly at the man and his fire extinguishers. Luckily the famous Cuneo mouse, which did not appear until 1953, was not there to distract her.

GIANTS REFRESHED

"PACIFICS" IN THE DONCASTER LOCOMOTIVE WORKS

PUBLISHED BY THE LONDON & NORTH EASTERN RAILWAY (A.R.1075)   PRINTED IN GREAT BRITAIN   WATERLOW & SONS LIMITED, LONDON & DUNSTABLE.

Royal Border Bridge, Berwick – c. 1946, 38" x 48" (poster 40" x 50")
This was Cuneo's second poster for the LNER. Railway engines
steaming across bridges are among Terence Cuneo's most
successful paintings and a whole series of these were done for
British Rail. Both this painting and the later Tay Bridge
share a similar lyrical quality. Preliminary sketches for the bridge
show Cuneo experimenting with at least two possible angles
from which to paint his composition. In one version, the artist
has chosen a straightforward side-on viewpoint; the other, his
eventual choice, is more dramatic with the powerful curve of the
bridge and rails bringing the steam engine thundering towards
the spectator, while the passing gulls swoop out of its way.

ROYAL BORDER BRIDGE
BERWICK-ON-TWEED

ON THE EAST COAST ROUTE BETWEEN ENGLAND AND SCOTLAND

21

The Tay Bridge – c. 1957, 36″ x 48″ (poster 40″ x 50″)

In this painting, Cuneo has again chosen a curving approach, with the powerful foreground girders of the bridge contrasting most effectively with the very painterly treatment of the water beneath. Partly obscured by the girder a steam train makes its way towards the town to be met by a more stolid diesel coming towards the viewer. The evening sky and dipping gulls give the scene a feeling of great tranquillity, with the smoke from the steam engine being echoed by the eddies in the river beneath.

However, Terence Cuneo's recollections of working conditions for the poster belie the peaceful appearance of the scene. Winds of almost forty miles per hour induced in him an almost trance-like state and it is to the great relief of his admirers that the artist did not plunge off the edge!

TAY BRIDGE
SEE SCOTLAND BY TRAIN

23

Glen Ogle – 1946, 38″ x 24″ (poster 40″ x 25″)

In this painting, Cuneo has captured the peaceful countryside feel of his Essex Mill painting, which had so attracted the publicity manager of the LNER. Instead of merely illustrating a steam locomotive correct to every last nut and bolt, the artist has chosen instead to show the scene almost from the vantage point of the engine herself and the lovely Highland glen forms the subject of the painting.

For the artist and his family the trip up to the far north was a refreshing change from the rigours of an increasing number of commissions, for it must be remembered that Cuneo by no means devoted his talents only to railway paintings, his repertoire extending from elaborate ceremonial to marvellously observed wild life paintings and, of course, horses.

Having first tried the Lochearnhead–Crieff line but failed to find what he was looking for, Cuneo turned to the Oban line and in particular the section through Glen Ogle. Seeing the rock which was to be placed almost in the centre of the finished painting, he knew he had found the compositional focus point for which he had been searching. Armed with his footplate pass, Cuneo then secured a ride with the lead engine of two 'Black Fives' needed to tackle the steep inclines. (The artist has always seized every opportunity to ride and even drive the locomotives which he was to portray, not only because of his love of steam but also to experience the true weight and strength of the beast.) Amidst appalling vibrations from the struggling engine, Cuneo waited for the rock to come into view and rapidly took a few photographs and several drawings of a scrawled nature. The next day he was able to return again in peace and quiet in order to make the necessary scenic studies and landscape notes. In the finished painting, the rock remains the central point with just half the boiler of the 'Black Five' visible on the right and some shocking pink flowers balancing the composition on the left.

GLEN OGLE
PERTHSHIRE

SEE SCOTLAND BY RAIL

ESSEX

TRAVEL BY RAIL

An L.M.S "BLACK 5" on GLEN OGLE

25

The Forth Bridge – 1952, 38″ x 48″ (poster 40″ x 50″)

Perhaps one of Cuneo's most arresting bridge pictures is the painting he did for British Rail of a streamlined A4 Pacific steaming across the famous Forth Bridge linking Clydeside and Fyfe. The relationship of steam, light and the rust red girders, whose lattice forms are reflected in the dappled water beneath, is quite masterly and brings to mind the Eiffel Tower paintings of Robert Delaunay. The way in which the locomotive has been allowed to be dominated by the complex diagonals of the mighty bridge makes for a most unusual and effective painting, which justifies all the pain and discomfort Cuneo endured when making rapid sketches for the painting the day that King George VI died in February 1952.

"Working conditions here were frankly terrifying. Although swaddled in flying suit, duffel coat, balaclava and mittens to say nothing of long woollen underwear . . . I was frozen. The screaming of the wind through the girders was so intense that trains, usually noisy on the bridge, passed beneath me in ghostly silence, their smoke snatched by the gale . . . Now my fingers became so numb that I could hardly hold a pencil. When finally the drawing was finished and I was ready to go down, a feeling of near panic took hold of me. One look down at the dark, surging water miles below, that appeared to race through the myriad lattice of the girders, had me in a sweat. Fixing my sketch-book on a string around my neck, I crawled on all fours along the cat-walk, descending the ladder down the great tubes with eyes tight shut, hoping nobody was around to witness my discomfort. When I did finally get to the bottom, I was shown the wind chart. I had been sketching in a 53 mile an hour gale!"

THE WORLD FAMOUS FORTH BRIDGE

SCOTLAND FOR YOUR HOLIDAYS

Services and fares from  stations, offices and agencies

The Day Begins – 1946, 30″ x 45″ (poster 40″ x 50″)

One of Cuneo's earlier paintings done for poster reproduction, was this painting of an LMS Pacific locomotive being prepared for work on shed. In an interesting article entitled 'Sunday Session' which appeared in *The Railway Gazette* in August 1947, the artist describes how the composition took shape:

"The theme was left to me, and after deliberation and considerable indecision, I decided on an interior of the Round Shed. There was something about that great shed, with its radiating tracks and quietly breathing locomotives that fascinated me. I spent a day planning and discussing arrangements, and generally getting things lined up for a start on the following Sunday morning. Sunday, because on that day the Round-shed would be as quiet as a church. (or so they told me!)"

Inevitably, things did not go according to plan (or one could say the best laid plans of mice and Cuneo go often times astray), in particular as the Class 7 'City of Hereford', star of the painting was nowhere to be seen. Assured that she would turn up later, another engine was proposed as a stand-in, but after much to-ing and fro-ing had got her into place, the 'City' herself steamed into view. Once she was in position, Cuneo felt his chosen viewpoint no longer worked and the artist spent many anxious minutes pacing round the shed watched by the assembled company. Further disturbances followed and, needing some two hours to finish, Cuneo was horrified to hear that his engine was about to leave in half an hour –

"Ye Gods, how I worked. In thirty minutes the drawing was as finished as I dared make it. I still had the colour note to do. With the engine crew hanging from the cab-side, and the entire Round-shed staff at my back, I scrawled frantic notes. A plume of steam roared from the safety valve, and the 'City' gave a warning toot on her whistle. I closed by my book with a snap and ran towards the table. A fleecy cloud of steam poured from the open cylinder cocks as the great wheels began to move. I grabbed a hand-rail and climbed into the cab as the engine trundled down the exit track. Slowly, through rain and gathering dusk, we wound our way to the end of the yards. The engine stopped at a group of dwarf signals just long enough for me to climb down. Then she was moving away again dissolving into the evening mist. My model, for the day."

None of the confusion and rush described above is apparent in the finished painting in which the locomotive, her steam pierced by slanting shafts of light from the roof, stands majestic and serene, while she is prepared for work. The fairly broad, impressionistic brush strokes used for the roof, smoke and light shafts reproduce extremely well in the poster and the diagonals of rails and light create a kind of halo around the engine, reinforcing the sense of weight and importance.

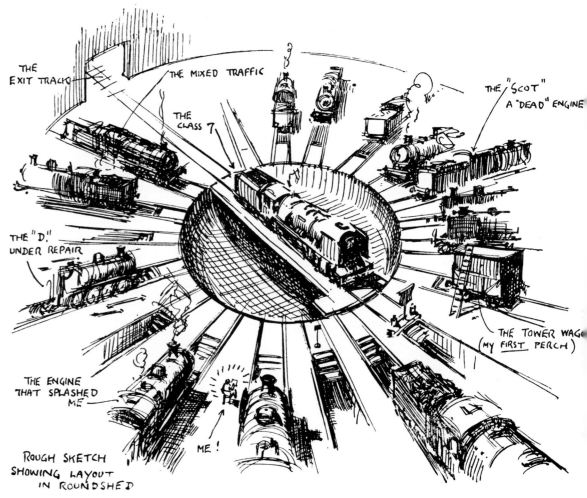

THE EXIT TRACK

THE MIXED TRAFFIC

THE "SCOT" A "DEAD" ENGINE

THE CLASS 7

THE "D." UNDER REPAIR

THE TOWER WAGON (MY FIRST PERCH)

THE ENGINE THAT SPLASHED ME

ME!

ROUGH SKETCH SHOWING LAYOUT IN ROUNDSHED

LMS THE DAY BEGINS

Lifting a 2-6-4 tank
Locomotive Erecting shops, Derby. (q.R. British Rlys.)

An Engine is Wheeled – 1949, 38" x 48"

It is interesting to compare this painting with the previous one painted some three years earlier. Where in the former, the locomotive seemed calm and mysterious, here all is hustle and bustle as nine men attend the lowering of the hefty 2-6-4 tank locomotive onto its wheels. The predominant colour notes of the painting are rust, cream and blue and their repetition on the engine being worked on at right and in the small figure in the middle distance at left help to give cohesion to the composition.

As often happened during the course of his railway commissions, when Cuneo arrived on the scene at Derby Locomotive works the engine was not in the state which he had envisaged. Planning to catch the moment when the body was reunited with its wheels, he found that the engine had already been replaced. However, the shed master was most obliging and simply raised the engine again to enable the artist to make the sketch reproduced above.

DERBY LOCOMOTIVE WORKS

AN ENGINE IS WHEELED

Clear Road Ahead – 1949, 38″ x 48″ (poster 40″ x 50″)

On occasion Cuneo has deserted the grand vista or complex composition in favour of a concentration on the men who make the mighty steam engines work – be they driver and fireman as here or the signalman of 'On Early Shift'. In order to achieve the real flavour and verisimilitude of the hot engine cab, Cuneo had the fireman dig a hole in the coals, from which vantage point he made the trip from Paddington to Reading at 70 miles per hour – not the easiest conditions under which to make a sketch! Whilst the fireman on the down trip made an excellent model, the engine driver was as animated as a block of wood and Cuneo had to wait for the return trip before he got the action and stance he required from another driver. Painted in broad chunky brush strokes, Cuneo has effectively captured the contrasting poses of the two men, the fireman full of vigour, the driver nonchalantly watching the line ahead, whilst above both their heads the rushing smoke enhances the impression of speed.

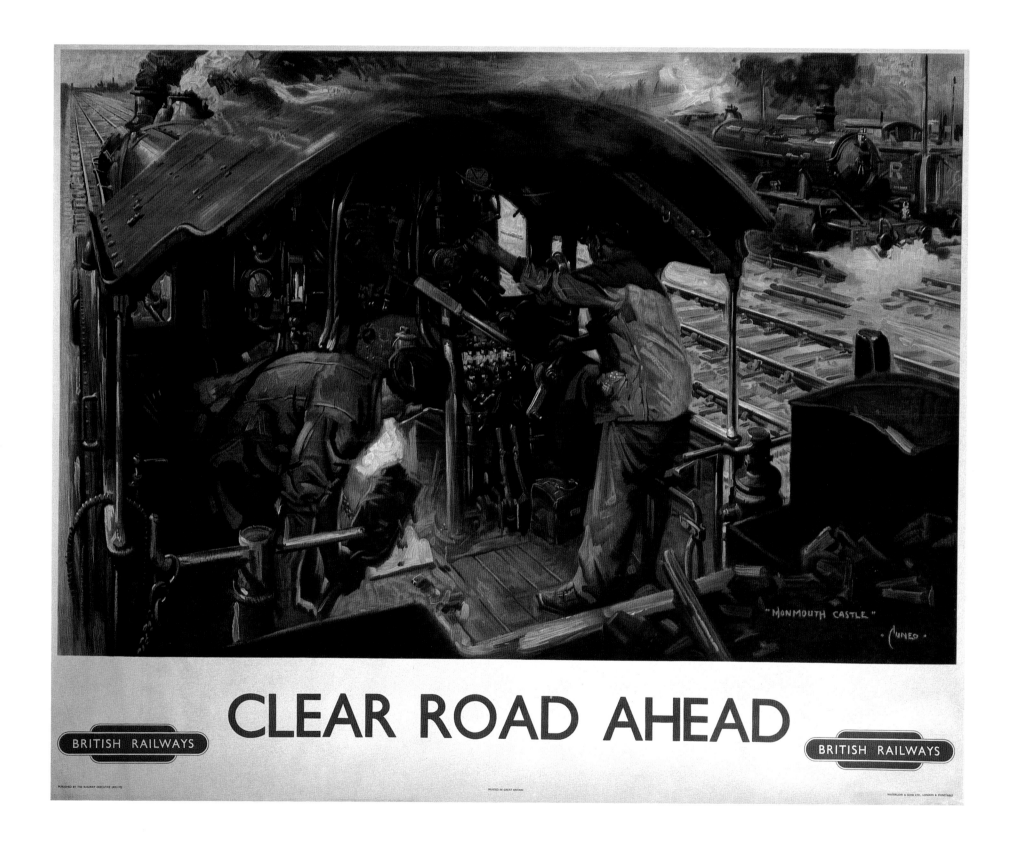

"MONMOUTH CASTLE"

CUNEO

CLEAR ROAD AHEAD

On Early Shift – 1948, 36″ x 45″ (poster 40″ x 50″)

In this composition, the main focus is the signalman – his head turned away, he watches intently the approaching A4 Pacific, leaning forward ready to pull the correct lever at the correct time. A comparison with the photograph, in which Cuneo can be seen sketching the scene, is most instructive as it shows clearly that the vitality of the finished work is quite lacking in the rather wooden pose of the signalman model. By painting the man from a different angle, with his jacket off and sleeves rolled up, one foot stepping forward, a sense of urgency and of getting down to work is immediately conveyed.

The sketch shows the detailed colour notes made by the artist and the vivid primaries on the lever shafts make for a bright and vibrant painting. Note too Cuneo's reminder to himself concerning the position and angle of the sun at a certain time of day. By choosing a time at which sunlight streams in, the artist has enlivened what is otherwise a rather dull and dingy signal box. Cuneo had earlier debated choosing the night shift, but obviously decided that this composition needed bright light and colours to bring it to life.

It was during work on this painting that Cuneo had the unpleasant experience of being caught in a tunnel, alluded to earlier in the text. Ever keen to research his work and needing references for another painting he was engaged upon, Cuneo rode with a friendly engine driver through the tunnel before being dropped off to walk back through. After one fast train had steamed by, Cuneo realised to his horror that the enveloping smoke had completely blacked out the tunnel and he could hear another train approaching:

"An ice-like hand seemed to grip me as I realised I hadn't a clue which way to move. In turning I had lost all sense of direction. But move I must. The coaches had gone and now the tunnel reverberated horribly to the oncoming train and a sudden draught buffeted my face. Noise was all around – everywhere; the very nearness of it seemed to numb my senses. I took a step in the darkness, then another. My toe struck something hard and I all but fell. One of the metals. Fine, but which one? I took a chance and with arm outstretched, stepped over the rail. Almost at once my hands came in contact with the wall. Thank God!"

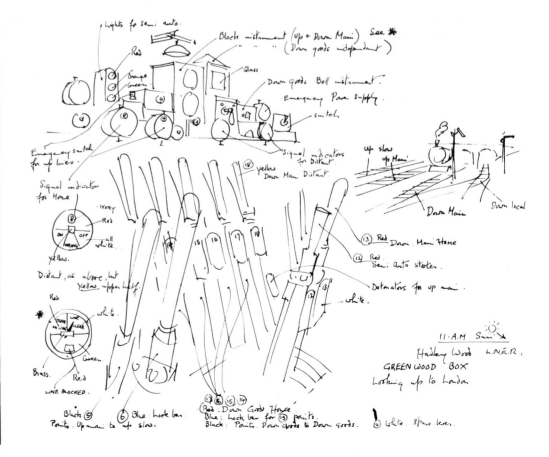

Forging Ahead – 1950, 33″ x 48″ (poster 40″ x 50″)

Unlike 'On Early Shift', the signal box features only partially in this painting, dating from the early 1950s, but it nevertheless provides an important framing element for the picture. Indeed, the artist so liked this position just outside Paddington station that he was to use it again some twenty or thirty years later for a private commission. In this painting, a BR 'Britannia' pulls out slowly and Cuneo has chosen a slightly high viewpoint achieved by clambering up onto a goods van. The painting is a study of light and shade falling on the engine and her steam, the latter being painted in quick, chunky strokes which fill the entire top right of the canvas, partly obliterating the road bridge behind. The figure at right seems unconcerned as the engine gets up steam and 'forges ahead' away from the city and towards the West Country beyond.

 **FORGING AHEAD**

Bon Voyage – 1952, 31″ x 48″ (poster 40″ x 50″)

Cuneo's poster commissions for British Rail were not confined to work on the English railway lines, and in 1952, Don Faulkner of the Southern Region took him to Calais to create a poster with an Anglo-French theme. Appropriately enough, both the English and French cross-channel steamers, 'Invicta' and 'Cote d'Azur', are docked and disgorging their passengers. The finished result was somewhat more complex than many of Cuneo's poster compositions, and reminiscent in feel of 'Loading for Export at Fords Dagenham' of 1946. (see page 55)

To capture the entirety of the scene Cuneo required a high vantage point and taking the initiative as soon as he got off the boat, he found a ladder and clambered up on to a wagon-lits to execute a quick sketch. Needless to say, almost immediately the train started to move off, leaving the artist to make an undignified descent into the arms of a waiting gendarme. Rescued from an irate customs officer by Don Faulkner, he then repaired to the Locomotive Depot and a static cattle truck in order to get some more peaceful and accurate engine details, seen in the sketch and photograph reproduced opposite. Despite all the trials and tribulations, the finished painting is marvellously evocative of the frenetic activity of Calais – the blue shirted dockers unloading baggage; the passengers pouring off the boat and onto the waiting train: the locomotive steam raised and ready to go; the swooping seagulls. . . .

The Royal Albert Bridge, Saltash – 1959, 38″ × 48″ (poster 40″ x 50″)

In 1959, Isambard Kingdom Brunel's famous bridge linking Devon and Cornwall across the river Tamar, celebrated its centenary. What better way to commemorate this event than by a Terence Cuneo poster? As a child going back to school Cuneo had hung from the window and watched the great tubes of the bridge float overhead and I must confess to a similar obsession. In particular, the sight of the bridge on the way down from school in Kent signalled the start of the holidays and being home at last.

In order to achieve the perfect spot, Cuneo had been given authority to travel on the footplate of the London train after it left Plymouth station and stop it exactly where he wanted for just 30 seconds. However, he was unable to find the desired angle and before finding the final position, he walked the bridge at dawn, during the day and even at night. In order to find a viewpoint which showed both the bridge and the water beneath, a position was chosen on the Cornish side and Cuneo clambered out to perch on one of the stone columns.

There is no doubt that all the exploratory work more than paid off, culminating in one of Cuneo's most memorable paintings. The golden light of the sky is reflected in the water below, the smoke is carried downwards by the wind allowing the name of the bridge's famous creator to stand out proud and clear, and on the river beneath a small tug chugs underneath on its way to the estuary beyond. It all seems so effortless, as it should do, with only the artist aware of the work behind a truly successful composition.

Study for "Royal Albert Bridge", Saltash Poster.

41

Track Laying by Night – 1950s, 33″ x 45″ (poster 40″ x 50″)

Throughout his career, Cuneo has often chosen to paint a particular scene at night in order to add an unusual dimension or create a more dramatic atmosphere.

As described by the artist, the preparatory work for this painting was executed under particularly chaotic conditions. Deluged by rain, the track-laying train and her crew worked rapidly, depositing their forty foot lengths of track and immediately moving on to the next spot. Cuneo was forced to work at the same pace and in his haste inadvertently cut his finger on a razor blade kept in his pocket for sharpening pencils. Nevertheless the sketches were done and the desired effect achieved. It is a composition where the track-layers are the main focus of interest and recalls nineteenth century genre paintings showing workers engaged in a range of manual tasks. In contrast, the locomotive, usually the heroine of the piece, has taken a lesser role and is barely visible at the left of the composition.

43

Night Freight – 1960, 36″ x 48″ (poster 40″ x 50″)

A particularly dramatic night composition is the appropriately named 'Night Freight' painted to show off British Rail's newly introduced diesel locomotives.

Here a BR diesel hauls 'Condor' and occupies the centre of the painting, framed at left by a passing steam locomotive, at right by a signal gantry. The artist has chosen a particularly low viewpoint right by the track and thus the viewer feels almost as if the engine is about to leap out of the dark. The deep blue of the freely painted sky broken up by puffs of steam and smoke in orange and white, the glowing lights and gleaming rails all contribute to the dramatic quality of the scene. In addition, the lack of any human figures, apart from the small face of the driver peering through the window of his mighty steed, increases the feeling of the engine as a living creature with a life and will of its own. Although, Cuneo's first love was and remains the steam locomotive, the painting illustrates his ability to invest the more mundane diesel with great power and strength.

Service to Industry – late 1950s, 36″ x 48″ (poster 40″ x 50″)

It is interesting to compare 'Night Freight' with this painting done for a poster aimed at showing British Rail's importance for industrial clients such as ICI. The painting is undated but the treatment of the sky and the low viewpoint would place it stylistically close in time to 'Night Freight'.

An engine steams slowly by at left while on the right a diesel is picking up or discharging its load. The loose slanting brushstrokes of the sky and smoke contrast well with the curve of the rails, and the composition is framed at right and above by the sides and top of a bridge.

SERVICE TO INDUSTRY

THE GREAT I C I CHEMICAL WORKS AT BILLINGHAM–ON–TEES DEPEND
ON BRITISH RAILWAYS FOR THE DELIVERY EACH YEAR OF NEARLY TWO
MILLION TONS OF COAL, 150,000 TONS OF OTHER COMMODITIES, AND FOR
THE DISPATCH OF THREE-QUARTERS OF A MILLION TONS OF FERTILISERS,
CEMENT, BULK LIQUIDS AND OTHER PRODUCTS.

BRITISH RAILWAYS

Signals – 1962, 31″ x 46″ (poster 40″ x 50″)

The object of the painting was, as its title suggests, to illustrate British Rail's new colour light signalling equipment.

It is for this reason, that the locomotives in this painting are secondary to the large signal gantry which stands proudly in the foreground. In addition, the artist obviously felt that a night scene would enhance the dramatic effect and show off the new electric lights to their best advantage.

49

Progress – 1957, 36″ x 48″

While on the theme of modernisation and diesels, it is interesting to illustrate this painting which was executed for the cover of Unilever's magazine *Progress* 1957–58 with the slogan 'Every week British Railways Modernisation Plan goes further ahead'. This plan drawn up in 1955 envisaged the complete replacement of steam by diesel traction and the painting illustrates the plan in action.

In composition, the painting recalls one of Cuneo's first British Railways commissions 'An Engine is Wheeled' painted at Derby Locomotive works. However, this time instead of the proud steam engine being the centre of attention, a diesel is being fitted with her engine, while at left another diesel at a lesser stage of completion awaits her turn. On the far right, the nose of a relegated steam engine pokes out, while at the back a much earlier steam engine still 'North Star', dating from the mid-nineteenth century, is raised up on a plinth almost like an exhibit in a museum. Here then we have 100 years of the railways captured in a marvellous composition. The triangular shapes of the glass roof of the locomotive works, only suggested in the earlier painting, are given full expression here and their light airiness is a telling contrast to the weight of the big diesels below.

Painted by Terence Cuneo for the cover of the Unilever magazine 'Progress' Winter issue 1957-8

PROGRESS

Every week British Railways Modernisation Plan goes further ahead

PUBLISHED BY THE BRITISH TRANSPORT COMMISSION 4100

PRINTED BY WATERLOW & SONS LIMITED LONDON AND DUNSTABLE

Clapham Junction – 1966, 38″ x 48″ (poster 40″ x 50″)

Painted in 1966, this painting in many ways represents one of the artist's most complicated and difficult compositions for British Rail. As Cuneo himself described it, Clapham was extremely daunting:

"... a veritable Grand Canyon of railway impedimenta. A vast area of tracks, points and crossovers, signal gantries, bridges and station platforms and out of this tangled medley I had to pick a view which would display the junction to its best advantage."

After trudging around all day looking for a vantage point, Cuneo finally found a spot on the signal gantry which he felt was ideal and sketching commenced. However, unlike many of his works in which the preliminary and more elaborate sketches will suffice, the artist took the canvas back to the site and painted on the spot. Getting all the right trains on the right tracks was a headache and upon asking the signalmen whether he had achieved this, Cuneo was horrified to learn that left as he had arranged things most trains would be involved in a multiple pile-up within a few minutes! Much re-positioning was required.

In the final version, two of Southern Railway's 'Light Pacifics', soon to be phased out, occupy centre stage, while to left and right an array of commuter trains come and go in a composition that is both satisfying aesthetically and correct technically – no mean achievement.

CLAPHAM JUNCTION

From the original oil painting by Terence Cuneo

SOUTHERN
BRITISH RAILWAYS

Loading for Export at Ford's Dagenham – 1946, 30″ × 40″

As has been recounted, after the Second War, Cuneo's career as a railway artist really took off, but it should not be forgotten that at the same time he was inundated with a multitude of other work by an enormous range of companies, the army and the government.

This painting is not really a railway painting as such, but it has been included on the basis of the small tank engine which can just be spotted puffing away amidst the mass of black Fords being loaded onto the ship.

The painting was one of Cuneo's first peacetime commissions and shows that his training during the war years of capturing a complex composition quickly and effectively had certainly paid off. One of the most important requisites for an artist is the ability to choose a good vantage point from which to create an interesting painting and here Cuneo has chosen a high angle enabling him to build the painting up into a pyramid shape with the boat as the apex towards which everything is inexorably drawn. The brushstrokes and colouring of this work are extremely attractive and impressionistic, particularly suited to paintings of light and water.

The Opening of the Stockton & Darlington Railway 1825

1949, 25" × 31"

This painting depicts 'Locomotion' with George Stephenson at the throttle as the train draws away from the horse drawn team she was to supersede and it illustrates the first time that any form of transportation had beaten the faithful horse.

The relatively small painting may be compared stylistically with Cuneo's painting 'The Mad English' of roughly a few months later and seems to hark back to his previous career as an illustrator of Boys' Annuals, lacking as it does the gravitas of some of his finest locomotive paintings. Nevertheless despite the lighthearted nature of the composition, Cuneo has made careful preparatory drawings, one of which is illustrated here.

CRAMP

The Mad English – 1950, 25″ x 30″

The previous painting, this work and the succeeding two are all part of a series illustrating the locomotive in competition with other types of motive power; firstly, the horse, here a 1906 Mercedes, later a 1920s Bentley and finally a modern sports car.

In this painting, the driver intoxicated with the possibilities of his new toy and recalling somewhat the character of Toad from 'Wind in the Willows', careers along, disturbing a flock of chickens, while the angry farmer and his dog chase after. The passenger clutches wildly at the driver's neck and the horse and cart bolt off. The exaggerated, almost caricature-like facial expressions and squawking chickens give the painting a humorous quality implied by its title. As with 'Stockton', Cuneo has taken great pains with the accuracy of the Crampton locomotive, although it is unlikely whether she would ever have run at the same period as the 1906 Mercedes.

← Bentley versus the Blue Train – 1970, 30″ x 40″

Some twenty years later, Cuneo was to return to this theme
again, inspired by an exploit in which he himself would love to
have taken part, appealing as it would have done to his sense of
fun and adventure.

On 13 March 1930 'Babe' Barnato bet his friend, whom he was
seeing off on the famous 'Blue Train' that he, Barnato, would
reach the coast first. Averaging 43.43 mph Barnato won his bet,
but was fined £160 as a result by the French Motor Racing
Authorities for taking part in an unauthorized race. In this
painting, the car is shown leading the train, while the ubiquitous
farmer on his horse-drawn cart turns round to stare in
amazement.

Peter Instone racing the Orient Express →

1986, 30″ x 40″

Last in the series of trains versus automobiles, is this amusing
painting in which Peter Instone and his Ferrari pass the Orient
Express near Innsbruck on the Austrian leg of the journey. While
the Stockton painting illustrates a momentous moment in
railway history, the last three paintings though separated in time
by a number of years, share the same light-hearted quality,
reflecting the lure of speed.

Interior of the Bar Car, Orient Express – 1985, 30″ x 40″

While on the subject of the Orient Express, it is appropriate to
include this interior painted by Cuneo during his trip on the
luxurious train. Cuneo has always been captivated by Venice,
the final destination of the current Orient Express, and the
combination of that city and the chance of a train ride was to
prove irresistible for him.

The First Days of Steam – 1954, 25″ x 30″

This painting and the following one, illustrate Richard Trevithick's famous Penydarren Tramroad locomotive in two different guises. The earlier version, painted in 1954, shows the locomotive steaming away from a bridge, whilst a LNWR single locomotive passes overhead. The painting is tranquil in feeling with the various vertical accents of the chimney, signal post and bridge pillasters being juxtaposed with the ovals and rounds of the massive fly wheel and the arch of the bridge.

The Penydarren Tramroad Locomotive

1963, 25″ x 30″

In contrast, the later version, commissioned for the Department of Industry by the late Richard Trevithick, M.I.C.E., great grandson of the inventor, captures the moment when the engine designed by his illustrious forebear successfully hauled a 10 ton load of bar iron and seventy passengers. The journey, which took place on 22 February 1804, was over nine and a half miles of tramroad between the ironworks and its loading point on the Glamorganshire canal in Abercynon. This was the first time a locomotive had ever drawn a load on rails and the task was accomplished in a time of 4 hours and 5 minutes.

In the painting, Richard Trevithick (1771–1833) is shown striding along just ahead of his creation, while a carpenter saw in hand is ready to remove any low branches which might impede the progress of the 'Iron Horse'. The preparatory sketches, one of which is included, were carried out at the Science Museum in London. The leaping dog by the front of the train contributes to a feeling of great liveliness and the painting as a whole can be compared with 'The Opening of the Stockton and Darlington Railway'.

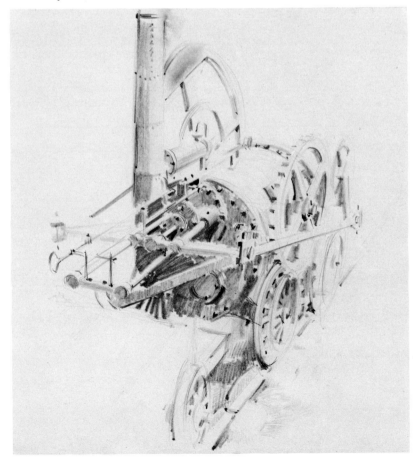

Triple Header in the Rockies – 1955, 30" x 20"

Apart from his commissioned works, Cuneo loves to paint for his own pleasure and on countless trips abroad, both on work and on holiday, he often sneaks off for a few hours or days to record a steam locomotive or two, or even, as shown in this photograph, to snatch the odd ride or drive. The two paintings illustrated here are perfect examples of simple yet effective and spontaneous work done on trips of this kind.

In the mid-1950s, Cuneo was commissioned to paint the Trans-Canada highway and this painting was executed at that time. So steep were the inclines in the Rocky Mountains that triple-heading with steam locomotives was often necessary to haul the heaviest trains.

The painting is uncomplicated yet wonderfully lively and arresting. The format is unusual for a railway painting and helps to reinforce the power of the towering mountain at left, while the smoke rises high in the clear mountain air. Note too the large, free brushstrokes used for the depiction of mountain and sky.

The Crossing, Broken Hill, Rhodesia – 1957, 17" x 22"

Cuneo has made fourteen trips to Zimbabwe, or Rhodesia as it then was, and this painting is a delightful momento of one of them. The artist was attracted by the contrast between the beauty of the blue jacaranda tree and the filthy black smoke. The lack of any extraneous details and the clear blue sky manage to convey the vast empty spaces of Rhodesia.

Loading Guinness on the Liffey, Dublin – 1956, 25″ x 30″

Commissioned by Guinness in Dublin and somewhat similar in feel to 'Loading Fords at Dagenham' of 1946, this painting is another treatment of a quayside railroad scene, captured so well by Terence Cuneo. While in the former work, the train is dwarfed by the cars, here the peculiar little tank engine almost looks like a barrel of Guinness herself.

To reach the quay the little trains ran under the road, and Cuneo recalled that, as ever anxious to research his subject thoroughly, he made a terrifying ride down the narrow spiralling track where to raise your head would have been to have it knocked off! The strongly receding diagonals are a most effective compositional device and in the left background can be glimpsed some of the very attractive Georgian houses flanking the river Liffey.

67

←The Pass Track, Ffestiniog Railway Wales

1958, 30'' x 40''

Ffestiniog Railway – November 1985, 30'' x 40''

The narrow gauge Ffestiniog Railway in North Wales began operations in 1863 and after a period of decline and closure is now enjoying a renaissance, thanks to the efforts of devoted preservationists. The gradients between Porthmadog and Blaenau Ffestiniog are very severe and in addition curves on the 1 foot 11.5 inch gauge track are very sharp. Thus small and strong engines are required.

These two paintings commissioned by the railway are separated in time by almost thirty years. In the earlier version, Cuneo chose one of the spots on the single track line where the small saddle tank 'Linda' could pass with another. Unfortunately when he turned up to sketch it was pouring with rain and much of the work had to be done from a parked car. During the course of executing his second commission, he made a return trip on 30 October 1985 and was given the chance to drive 'Linda', the model for his first painting.

Grooming the Diesels – March 1960, 40" x 30"

Painted at the locomotive sheds outside King's Cross, this painting shows one of the newly-introduced Type 4 diesel locomotives. Whilst in other paintings depicting diesels, a stray steam engine has managed to get herself into the canvas, here modernity holds total sway.

It is interesting to recall that in 'Night Freight' Cuneo had also chosen a similarly low view point and he obviously felt, quite rightly, that this was a position that shows off these flat-nosed machines, to their best advantage.

The March Hare – 1962, 20″ x 30″

Executed in Northern Spain, this small painting shows Cuneo in playful mood as his 0-4-2 steam locomotive just fails to overtake the speeding hare. Barely discernible some yards behind the hare is a racing mouse!

In fact, the preparatory sketches for this painting were done in the shunting yards at Valladolid, where Cuneo came upon the small engine and spent several happy hours sketching her. The completely side-on depiction of locomotives as seen here is comparatively rare in Cuneo's work as they are usually angled to present a three-quarters view or often presented full-face.

sketch for "Evening Star"
Southall shed.

Evening Star – 1963, 30″ x 40″

This painting shows the famous '9F' 2-10-0 locomotive 'Evening Star' steaming by in classic Cuneo style. She was the last steam locomotive to be constructed for British Railways, part of a group of locomotives which were introduced too late in the age of steam and some of which went to the scrapyard after only six years' service. Fortunately, this fine example was spared such a fate, having been preserved in the National Collection.

Cuneo has chosen to portray her from a low, lineside position and the locomotive steams majestically towards the viewer crowned by plumes of smoke and steam. The first sketch for the painting was made at Southall Shed, scene of many of Cuneo's research trips, and shows the artist establishing the basic shapes such as the rounds of the wheels, boiler and pistons, before adding all the details at a later stage. This painting was used by Tri-ang Hornby as the cover for one of their catalogues.

On a frivolous note, it is worth mentioning that the painting is notorious for the difficulties it has caused to those wishing to play 'spot the mouse' (for the answer please turn to page 160)! The mouse was first introduced by Terence Cuneo in 1953 and has been an added amusement for admirers of his work ever since. Those readers wishing to pursue the subject further should refer to the artist's autobiography *The Mouse and His Master*.

Cuneo
October 1963

Southern Tank – 1966, 40″ x 30″

The model for the painting (an ex-LSWR Drummond M7) had to be ignominiously dragged from its shed by a diesel shunter! However, in the final painting she looks cheerful enough and the plume of smoke contrasts well with the shocking pink flowers of the rosebay willowherb growing alongside the track.

As with the 'Evening Star', this painting was also used for a Tri-ang catalogue cover.

The Black Prince – 1974, 30″ x 40″

Like 'Evening Star' this locomotive is a '9F' 2-10-0 and was the last steam locomotive to haul a commercial train for British Rail. Here the 'Prince' is being driven by the late Sir Richard Summers, formerly a director of the LMS railway.

Unlike the more classic pose adopted for 'Evening Star', here Cuneo has chosen to come in very close on the engine herself and indeed, she fills almost three-quarters of the painting with her mighty bulk creating an unusual and effective composition.

The locomotive was saved from the scrap heap by David Shepherd, another well-known railway artist, who bought her from BR in 1967 and she is now installed on his East Somerset Railway. The photograph shows Terence Cuneo and David Shepherd together with a tank engine.

Double Header in the Highlands – 1968, 28″ x 36″

Here Cuneo depicts two of the LMS Class Fives 4-6-0s, or 'Black Fives' pulling freight up a steep incline. Designed by William Stanier and first introduced in 1934, these sturdy locomotives were extremely versatile and so successful that some 842 were produced over a seventeen year period. As the last British main-line steam operations were on former LMS lines, this helped many to survive after their younger sisters such as the '9Fs' had preceded them to the scrapyard.

Cuneo was among their many admirers having ridden the footplate of many such engines in the Highlands, while carrying out research for his 'Glen Ogle' poster and other Scottish paintings.

The snowy scene with its overcast sky and dark shadows provides a perfect foil for these powerful workhorses and there is no doubt that Cuneo's depiction of trains in the snow are among his finest works.

The Track, Paddington – 1969, 20″ x 30″

As its title implies, the gleaming rails are indeed the main subject of this painting and the yellow-faced 'Western' class 52 seems almost incidental in comparison.

The low, lineside vantage point from which the painting has been done, and from where the Paddington road bridge makes a strong, architectural feature, was a favourite one with the artist. However, while in other works involving steam locomotives such as the British Rail poster 'Forging Ahead', steam and smoke partially obscure the bridge, it is seen here in all its clarity. This work quite accidentally falls into the photo realist school of painting and is a minor masterpiece of its kind.

The Old Red Caboose, Albert Canyon, Canada
1969, 30″ x 40″

Revelstoke Depot – c. 1978, 25″ x 30″ →

It is interesting to compare these two Canadian paintings separated in time by some ten years. Both feature the old red caboose, which is given greater prominence in the earlier painting of the same name, but is still discernible in the second. The rusty red of the old caboose contrasts effectively with the bluish purple of the mountains behind, their peaks capped with snow.

Comparison of these paintings with the charcoal sketch reproduced at right, suggests that Cuneo has dipped into an old sketchbook for inspiration and in order to ensure the accuracy of the caboose and steam train. In the earlier painting the relationship of the two has much in common, with the painting being in effect a mirror image of the drawing. Thus, throughout his career Cuneo's sketchbooks have been able to serve as his very own reference library.

The photograph shows the artist sketching from the top of a box car in Montreal, Canada.

A King at Hereford – 1969, 30″ x 40″

This train, which includes the beautifully restored GWR monarch 'King George V', the 1951 Festival of Britain vestibule coach 'Aquilla', the dining car, bar, coach museum and cinema coach, was leased at the time to the Bulmer's cider company. It occasionally made short journeys of ¾ of a mile, in the course of which an excellent lunch would be served for special guests as the train slowly travelled back and forth throughout the duration of the meal with varying effects on the passengers' digestion!

First introduced in 1927, the four cylinder 'Kings' were the most powerful 4-6-0s ever to run in Britain. This particular locomotive made a trip to the USA in 1927, having been chosen to represent the GWR and Britain at the centenary of the Baltimore and Ohio Railway. Much to his delight, Terence Cuneo had a chance to drive the locomotive during the execution of this painting. The 'King' has recently been removed from this site and placed back in the care of the National Railway Museum.

Compositionally the three gas towers behind the engine make for an unusual background; their squat rotundity echoing and almost dwarfing the steam locomotive. In the far distance can be glimpsed the spires of Hereford Cathedral.

The accompanying photograph, taken by the late Rev. Eric Treacy, the Bishop of Wakefield, shows Cuneo at work on the early stages of the painting. Note how firstly, only the rough outlines and position of gas towers and locomotive are delineated. Then the artist moves on to fill in and establish the volume of the locomotive boiler and her wheels. Once these major components are established correctly, work can continue on the rest of the painting.

The Britannia Bridge – 1970, 36" x 50"

This painting shows an LMS re-built 'Royal Scot' working the Irish Mail and steaming majestically over Robert Stephenson's beautiful Egyptian-style bridge spanning the Menai straits in North Wales. In 1970, a terrible fire almost completely destroyed the bridge and shortly afterwards, the late Sir Richard Summers of Shotton Steel Works commissioned Cuneo to paint the bridge before it was totally demolished.

The original 'Royal Scot' class was first introduced in 1927, but was substantially rebuilt from 1943 onwards and in fact virtually only the cab, wheels and some ancillary equipment remained from the earlier version.

Walking through the ruins, Cuneo eventually found the perfect spot – the point where the locomotive emerges from between the two massive stone lions. The normally, large locomotive is here dwarfed by their stately bulk. The finished painting shows no signs of the ravages of the fire and its aftermath, as Sir Richard desired a memorial of the bridge in all its Victorian glory.

Castle on the Coast – 1970, 24″ x 41″

Here Terence Cuneo recreates a childhood memory of the Dawlish to Teignmouth stretch of the GWR mainline. Coming home from school, he would eagerly await the appearance of the 'Old Man Rock' glimpsed as the train rushed out of one tunnel before plunging into another. It is one of four versions of steam at Dawlish which appear in this book and the subject obviously appeals compositionally as well as emotionally. Indeed, the image of a train emerging from a tunnel is both dramatic and economic, avoiding the problems of painting the whole length of a train and allowing the artist to concentrate on the central core of the painting – the locomotive herself.

Here we see the 4-6-0 'Monmouth Castle' upon which Cuneo had ridden while making his sketches for the poster 'Clear Road Ahead'. The 'Castles' were introduced in 1923 and quickly established a reputation of being economical and fast, eclipsing rival LMS machines when 'Launceston Castle' ran on their lines in 1926. There is little doubt that they were one of the great locomotives of the age of steam.

Choosing a high viewpoint, the artist has contrived to capture both the engine and the dramatic Dawlish coastline. The red cliffs curve away to the right and their diagonals mirror those of the track running strongly from left to right.

91

Emerging from the Tunnel – South Wales Pullman

1973, 25″ x 30″

In contrast to the previous painting, Cuneo's use of the tunnel in this painting is much less dramatic and important. Furthermore the train is running through a cutting and there is a lack of any extraneous detail, both of which create a completely different atmosphere – one of calm rather than excitement.

Instead of the high viewpoints of the Dawlish paintings, Cuneo employs one of his favourite positions down on the track to further enhance the sheer weight and bulk of the locomotive.

Portrait of a Tank Engine – 1973, 20″ x 24″

This little Italian 0-4-0 tank was spotted pottering about the docks and rail yards in the Ethiopian Red Sea port of Massawa. Once again, Cuneo on holiday can turn away from the portrayal of great English expresses to revel in the hot Southern light and locomotives which are insignificant in themselves but charming as subjects for an informal portrait.

As we have seen elsewhere in his work, Cuneo frequently uses architectural elements to echo or reinforce the shape of the particular locomotive in question. Thus, here, the rectangular shape of the cab and side tanks is picked up in the simple white shapes of the buildings behind. Luxuriant vegetation is juxtaposed with the solidity of the engine, while the shunter with his white headgear and green flag lends an additional exotic note.

The Mightiest of the Mighty – 1973, 40" x 50"

A Union Pacific 'Big Boy' takes on coal and water at Harriman, Wyoming, before tackling the heavy grades of Sherman Hill. Introduced in 1941, these 4-8-8-4, 594 ton locomotives were the largest ever built and were the equivalent of four conventional engines. New track had to be laid to cope with their great weight and new turntables for their length. In all, 201 were built of which six remain today.

As a connoisseur of steam locomotives worldwide, it was inevitable that Cuneo would be unable to resist the depiction of such an exceptional machine: "To me these 6,000 horse power giants represent the ultimate in might and majesty and for the railroads of America they surely symbolize the final magnificence in steam motive power." However, even such power is not immortal and in 1957, the Union Pacific Railroad brought in new gas turbines and diesels for use on the hill.

Terence Cuneo borrowed a model belonging to his friend, David Garnock, in order to assist in the correct position of the elaborate pipework and valve gear. It is the night setting, however, which gives the painting its power and strength. Lit only from the right, its far side obscured and its headlight illuminating the steam and smoke, 'Big Boy' is majestic indeed. Cuneo has eliminated all unnecessary detail in this painting and come in close on the engine. Only the backlit water towers and coal chute at right are allowed to remain and their dark shapes help reinforce the drama and excitement of the painting.

Northbound Freight – *1975, 20″ x 30″*

Cuneo travelled for miles on the footplate of this great CNR diesel with the thermometer sometimes registering as much as 38 degrees below freezing.

To emphasize the impression of vast, open space and solitude, he has left the foreground deliberately bare with only the level crossing signs casting their mauvish-blue shadows across the snow. The locomotive, usually centre stage in his work, has been pushed back to the middle distance. However, she loses none of her presence in the process, towering over the two small figures at left and the small cluster of buildings at right. The clear sky, purple shadows and expanse of the white, crunchy snow capture perfectly the bright, dry air of the region.

The Sole Survivor, Soltau Shed, West Germany

1975, 30" x 40"

As usual when working abroad on other subjects, which in Germany are habitually military scenes, Cuneo managed to slip away in search of steam locomotives and discovered this veteran locomotive languishing in Soltau Shed.

Pictorially, Cuneo has returned to the theme of the engine in her shed, used to such effect in such classic railway posters of the late 1940s as 'An Engine is Wheeled' or 'The Day Begins'. The juxtaposition of light and dark, weight versus insubstantiality is always telling. A few shafts of light filter through the cavernous roof, and, although rusty and unloved, the might of the engine is revealed. Under Cuneo's loving brush, she seems eager to burst forth from the confines of her shed to start work again.

101

The Flying Scotsman, Half-way between Edinburgh and London – 1975, 30″ × 40″

This painting was commissioned by Bill McAlpine, the locomotive's present owner, as he particularly wanted a view of the famous locomotive as it passed the half-way point of its 392.9 mile journey. In 1888, the 'Flying Scotsman' had won the 'Race to the North' and in May 1928, competition between the East and West Coast lines having arisen anew, the 'Flying Scotsman' secured the world record for the longest non-stop run.

These LNER 'A3' 'Pacifics' designed by Nigel Gresley (later Sir Nigel) were introduced as 'A1s' in 1922 and later modified, improved and re-designated as 'A3s' in 1927. This particular locomotive No. 4472 is undoubtedly the most famous of its class and in the hands of Bill McAlpine it continues to run today. The artist has painted the 'Scotsman' several times during his career, another notable painting being 'The Flying Scotsman on the Forth Bridge'.

In this portrayal, Cuneo has enlivened the otherwise flat landscape by including another locomotive at right, which is dwarfed as the LNER express steams by at speed on her way to Edinburgh.

102

Maintenance on Shed, Germiston, South Africa

1976, 25" x 30"

Terence Cuneo has made numerous visits to South Africa and Zimbabwe, commissioned by the Anglo-American Corporation to paint their various mining interests.

In this painting, the architectural elements of the shed have, atypically, been kept to a minimum. Surrounded by swirling steam and smoke, the tough-looking engines are the only substantial elements in the painting. The colour scheme is similarly restrained with notes of red, green and purple contrasting effectively with the predominantly sombre tones of the painting as a whole.

The leading watertank of the Garratt locomotive in the foreground is immediately recognizable. Note that in the early 1950s, only one head-lamp was used unlike the smaller paired ones introduced later. Garratts were the principal heavy duty freight movers employed in South Africa.

Storm over Southall Shed – *1978, 18″ x 26″*

Although small, this painting is full of force as the two locomotives stand ready for departure, a Prairie tank in the foreground, a Mogul behind.

Many of Cuneo's most powerful paintings depict storm or night scenes and the vertical elements of water pipes and lamp posts frame the engines tightly as if confining them momentarily before they leap into action.

THE DUCHESS OF HAMILTON
No. 46229

The Duchess of Hamilton – 1978, 30″ x 40″

Terence Cuneo has often sought assistance from museums in his endeavour to achieve accuracy and verisimilitude. For this painting, the National Railway Museum at York brought the engine out from the museum, all newly painted and gleaming after her restoration.

Designed by William Stanier and modified by Tom Coleman, the 'Duchess' class 'Pacifics' were first introduced in 1937. Many were fitted with an aerodynamic casing such as the 6220 'Coronation'. However, after enthusiasm for streamlining had cooled, the next batch including this locomotive were without the casing. Perhaps the finest British designed 'Pacific', the 'Duchess of Hamilton' is in use today for special excursion work.

Cuneo has painted several versions of her and in this particular example, after a detailed drawing had been made on site, the landscape was added at a later stage. The angle of the locomotive has also been changed, from the flat ground outside the museum to a steeper Pennine incline.

↓ Sunset of An Era – 1970s, 30″ x 40″

Locomotives Waiting to Enter the Depot, Boulogne↘
February – 1979, 30″ x 40″

These paintings show two aspects of the Depot at Boulogne. In 'Sunset of An Era' Cuneo portrays a lively scene with three locomotives preparing to depart, while 'Locomotives . . .', in which the left hand side of the canvas is quite bare, captures the bleakness of Northern France in the last days of steam operation.

They also display Cuneo's ability to capture the spirit of locomotives of any nation, be they British, South African, Canadian or French, and explain the reason for his great international appeal.

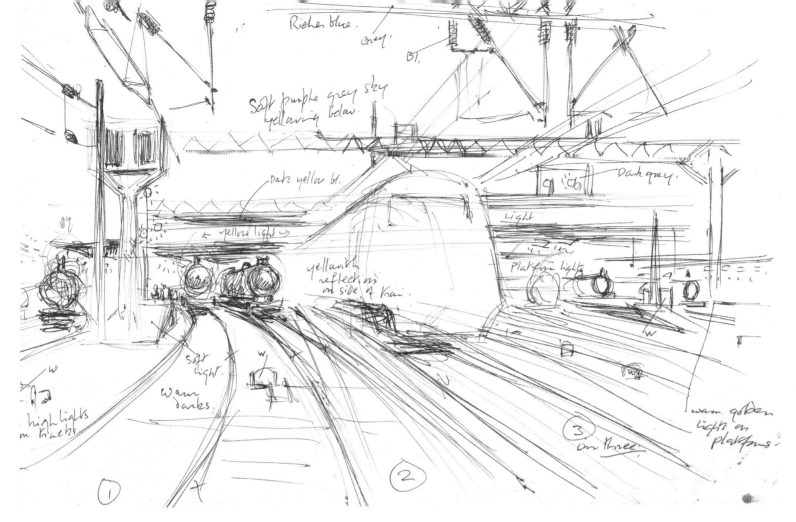

Into the '80s – The APT – 1979, 38″ x 40″

The painting on page 113 was commissioned for British Rail by Sir Peter Parker and was required to symbolize a glorious future in which the APT surges forward, leaving the ghosts of the steam train and earlier diesels behind. The striking wedge shape and vibrant yellow of the APT reinforces this image, while the five steam engines and one diesel who lurk behind seem drab in comparison.

As recounted by the artist, there were several stages in carrying out the preparatory work. First a day was spent drawing the APT in her shed, to be followed by drawings done on location at Euston. As dusk deepened into night, gauging which way the points had changed and where the next train would be coming from became increasingly difficult. Indeed, two 'minders' had to be on hand to lift Cuneo from the paths of moving trains – all part of the hazards of absorbing the atmosphere of the chosen location!

The preparatory drawings are very illuminating. The first two show Cuneo's detailed colour notes, while the third shows the compositional forcelines which will form the hidden structure of the finished painting and will ensure the total dominance of the APT.

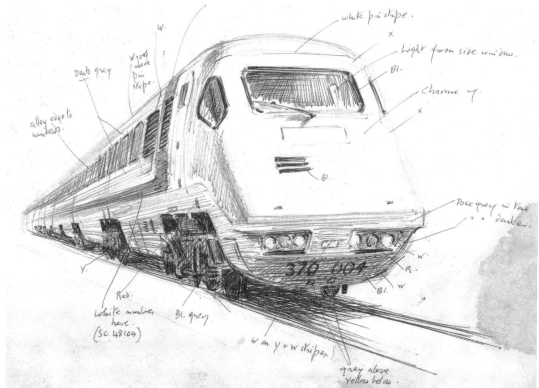

First compositional "rough" for the Euston Poster INTO THE 80's.

The Stamps

To coincide with the 150th anniversary of the Great Western Railway in 1985, the Royal Mail decided it would be a good opportunity to issue a set of five stamps depicting famous British trains, utilizing paintings by Terence Cuneo, with two stamps featuring the GWR, and one each for the LMS, the LNER and the SR.

The photograph shows Terence Cuneo signing First Day Covers in one of the pullman carriages of the Venice–Simplon Orient Express which that day made a special journey from Paddington to Didcot. He is watched from the platform by a woman who during the war saved him from a fire. At the time Cuneo was ill in a wooden military hospital with chicken pox and asleep did not sense the fire. The two had not met for some forty years!

The Tunnel – 1972, 30″ × 40″ →

The first painting in the series shows the moment when the famous 'Cornish Riviera' train hauled by 'King Richard III' emerges from one of the many tunnels on the stretch of line between Dawlish and Teignmouth. This express route was inaugurated on 1 July 1904 when the non-stop journey of 245.7 miles from Paddington to Plymouth took a mere four hours, thereby setting the world record for the longest daily non-stop run.

Unlike other paintings featuring this stretch of coast, Cuneo has not chosen to show the sea, apart from the spray of a few waves lapping at the stone sea wall, and the extremely high angle is a most unusual and difficult one from which to effectively paint a railway locomotive.

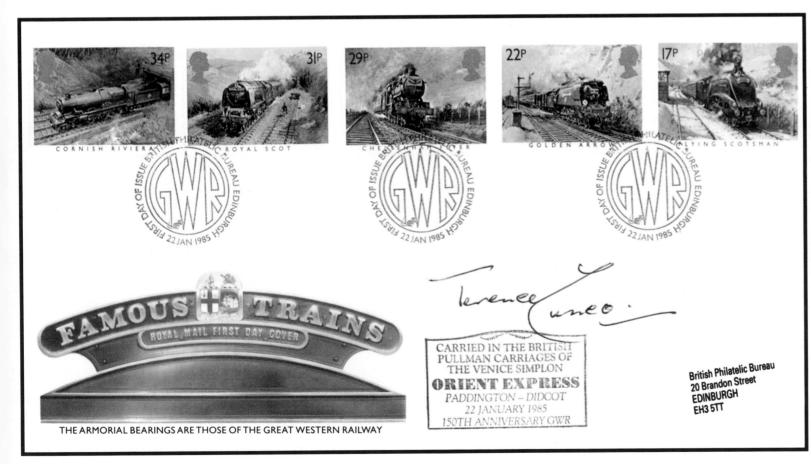

The Royal Scot – c. 1984, 20″ x 30″
The LMS 'Royal Scot' is seen being hauled by the 'Duchess Pacific' class 'City of Lancaster'. As the great rival to the 'Flying Scotsman' service, the 'Royal Scot' would leave Euston at 10 a.m. and after stopping at Rugby and dividing at Crewe, she would reach Glasgow and Edinburgh at 6.15 p.m.

The Cheltenham Flyer – 1981, 25″ x 30″

Here the 'Cheltenham Flyer' is pulled by locomotive No. 5069 the 'Castle' class 'Isambard Kingdom Brunel'. The train, pulled by a different locomotive, achieved its fastest run on 6 June 1932, when the 77.3 miles from Swindon to Paddington were covered at an average of 81.68 mph with a maximum speed of 92.3 mph.

The Golden Arrow – 1984, 21″ x 31″

The 'Golden Arrow' train, hauled by a 'Battle of Britain Class' 'Light Pacific' '219 Squadron' is shown in the vicinity of Dover, identifiable by the chalky white soil of the cutting. The Golden Arrow service linking England and France via Dover and Calais was introduced in 1929 and was finally withdrawn in 1972.

The Flying Scotsman – 1984, 22″ x 31″

The 'Flying Scotsman' is seen steaming through a snowy landscape hauled by the LNER 'A4' streamlined 'Pacific' 'Sir Nigel Gresley'.

The daily express first began its journeys in June 1862 and soon gained its famous nickname which was officially adopted by the LNER in 1923. The 'Race to the North' between the East and West Coast companies was a feature before the turn of the century and was won by the Great North Railway on 31 August 1888 in a time of 7 hours 26¾ minutes.

Much publicity was generated by the stamps commission and the photograph shows Cuneo standing on the incoming 'Sir Nigel Gresley' waving a vastly oversized stamp.

Mallard – 1980, 25" x 30"

Here Cuneo depicts another of the surviving streamlined 'A4' Pacifics, 'Mallard'. The streamlining was introduced in 1935 in response to admiration expressed by LNER directors for the German 'Flying Hamburger' streamlined train. The shape apparently upset many purists at the time, although today in our eyes it may seem the epitome of speed, modernity and stylish excellence.

Cuneo has painted 'Mallard' several times, but from this angle, the full impact of the dramatic smoke-box styling is particularly well emphasized.

←Freight East from Pietermaritzburg – 1980, 30″ x 40″

South African Freight – 1982, 14″ x 22″

In these two paintings, Cuneo has returned to South Africa, where the strong sun and dramatic shadows have always had great appeal for him. Both show him using a strong, rich palette not always possible in capturing the softer, greyer hues of the British countryside.

The locomotive in the 1980 painting is one of the very distinctively shaped Beyer-Garratts. Most of these patented locomotives were built by Beyer-Garratt in Britain, but some were manufactured by Raismes in France for the PLM on their Algerian routes. Later many of these enjoyed long service in South Africa. The cabs were fitted with duplicate controls at the rear to facilitate reverse running.

Cuneo has cleverly placed the locomotive between two tall trees to concentrate attention on its mighty bulk and the setting sun and dark black smoke make this a very dramatic painting.

Similarly, in 'South African Freight' Cuneo has painted the scene bathed in a late afternoon light, which is juxtaposed with the deepening shadows of the rocky gorge, through which the '14 CRB' winds its way. The three predominant colours of purplish blue, reddish brown and gold have been used with great economy and to great effect.

Preparation for Departure, Southall Shed – 1981, 30" x 40"

This painting is very similar in location, composition and feel to 'Storm over Southall Shed' on page 107. However in this composition another locomotive has been added, and the weight of the three boilers across the canvas creates a triple echo effect. Furthermore, the foreground area has been reduced and the painting transformed into a night scene.

The railway workers give a sense of scale of these huge monsters about to speed into the night, while the contrast between areas of light and dark, make this a dramatic and impressive painting.

Cuneo has recalled how he spent many hours at Southall Shed both by day and night, making studies for this painting and others.

Stabling for the Little Giants – 1982, 20″ x 30″

Both drawing and painting represent a scene from the Darjeeling railway much beloved by Terence Cuneo. While the drawing shows a relatively close-up view of the little engine with its curiously shaped boiler, in the painting she has been moved to the background. Indeed, the artist has given equal importance to the group of colourfully depicted adults and children in the foreground, and Cuneo's skill as a portrait painter is used to great effect in these informal studies of people in everyday poses.

"ON SHED"
DARJEELING RAILWAY
OCT. 1981.

127

Black Five Taking on Water at Speed 1983, 30″ x 40″

In this painting, Cuneo returns to one of his favourite
locomotives, the 'Black Five', on this occasion giving her the
setting of golden, autumnal sky. The water spraying out from
the tender and the locomotive's flattened smoke help to create
an impression of great urgency. It is amusing to recall Cuneo's
anecdote in which the driver of one such locomotive confided
that so rough was the ride in the cab of a 'Black Five' that on
particularly bad stretches they would take out their teeth and put
them in their pockets before "the engine bloody well knocks
them out of our heads for us"!

The Last German Steam Engine in service

1984, 12″ x 16″

In comparison with the calm isolation and strength of the
'Express', this small tank engine has a lighthearted air, with
pipes and lights seemingly attached to every part of her body.
Puffing away contentedly, she seems to enjoy the ministrations
of her two blue-overalled minders! This is a charming little 'portrait'
which recalls such works as 'The March Hare' on page 73.

A Winter Express – 1982, 16″ x 24″
Here a German DB BR 01 steams through a wintery landscape in
a classic Cuneo composition. The illusion of movement has been
created almost entirely through the juxtaposition of fluid areas of
light and shade in the smoke and on the snow, against the static
trees at the right of the painting.

Last of the Giants – 1985, 30" x 40"

As with his painting 'Sole Survivor' of 1975, this painting was squeezed in whilst carrying out a commission for the Royal Artillery.

With this depiction of the 2-10-0 steam locomotive Terence Cuneo has captured the very essence of long-freight trains trundling across Europe. Here speed has been arrested and the leisurely portrayal of the exhaust and the way in which the steam from the draincocks and cylinders swirls gently out, reinforces the feeling that this giant, at least, is in no hurry to depart the scene.

Firefly Emerging from Box Tunnel – 1985, 30" x 40"
From time to time, Cuneo enjoys a return to painting a locomotive from the very early days of steam traction, in this case 'Firefly'. It is interesting to compare this painting with a much earlier sketch for a Bury-built locomotive and it is quite possible that this may have been the starting point for this work.

The Helensburgh Electric Railcar – 30″ x 40″

This was another commission for British Rail, executed in the early 1960s and made into a poster. It represents a suburban electric train linking Helensburgh and Glasgow.

Docklands Light Railway – 1987, 40″ x 30″ →

It has been seen that whilst Cuneo might prefer to paint a classical steam locomotive, he can turn his brush to the protrayal of any railway locomotive. Here he tackles a very contemporary scene, capturing the bright red and blue Docklands Light Railway as it carries commuters to and from the city. The extensive development of the Docklands area can be glimpsed in the background.

In its general feel and composition this painting has certain affinities with the much earlier Helensburgh Electric Railcar.

Bridge 70a. Brinnington, Stockport – 1988, 40″ x 30″

This painting, while not strictly speaking a railway painting, has been included because it portrays the final installation of an important new railway bridge. Furthermore, it shows Cuneo tackling a complex composition that can be favourably compared with many of his earlier industrial paintings.

Commissioned by Bill Summers, Cuneo first visited the site by day and could not at first see how to create a dramatic composition. However, having insisted on re-visiting the bridge at night, he was delighted to find the subject transformed into an object of power and mystery. The moment the bridge, spanning the M66 was in place, 'Mallard' was run over it at speed.

It is interesting to compare Cuneo's dramatic treatment of the bridge with the painting by K. Hick in which the latter's approach is more typical of such civil engineering projects.

Mallard – 1987, 30″ x 40″

In 1987, Terence Cuneo was commissioned to paint 'Mallard' in order to commemorate the 50th anniversary, the following year, of the time when on 3 July, 1938, the locomotive captured the world record for steam traction, attaining a speed of 126 mph. At the same time, this commission was also a personal tribute to the artist as the ensuing print was published on 1 November, 1987, the artist's 80th birthday. Tremendous interest was generated by this commission and Cuneo's progress on the painting was the subject of a documentary by Central television.

It is interesting to compare this painting of 'Mallard' with a previous portrayal from 1980 (page 121). The earlier painting is more formal and controlled, whereas this later work is more expressionistic in feel; the totally flattened exhaust conveying the tremendous speed attained by the engine during her record breaking run.

Although now an octogenarian, Cuneo's enthusiasm for his subject remains undimmed and the 1988 and 1989 have seen many new canvases in which he takes up a familiar theme to produce something new and fresh.

Dawlish – "The Old Man Rock" – 1989, 30" x 40" →

The Sea Wall – 1988 18" x 24"

In these two paintings, Cuneo has returned to one of his favourite stretches of the line traversed by the 'Cornish Riviera', that between Dawlish and Teignmouth.

'The Sea Wall' shows the 'down' train steaming merrily along, her fireman waving to two figures on the beach, while Cuneo's latest painting has set the scene at night with the GWR 'King' class locomotive on its way back to London. The distinctive rock is visible to the left of the engine silhouetted against a dark blue sky, the moon casts the shadow of the locomotive onto the chippings, while the only other illumination is provided by the sparks flying out as the fireman shovels in coal. This painting is as dramatic as the former is calm.

A Country Halt – 1987, 16″ x 20″ →

↓ A Local Pulls Out – 1987, 20″ x 24″
These two paintings both depict charming rural scenes in which local trains are observed going happily about their business.

'A Country Halt' captures a typical scene from the GWR of some thirty years ago, whilst in 'A Local Pulls Out' the scene has been transferred to France. Both paintings are reminiscent of the Ffestiniog railway paintings and show Cuneo being equally at home on small branch lines as the grander tracks beaten by the glamorous expresses.

← The Long Drag, USA – 1987, 24" × 30"

↓ The Storm, Big Boy on Sherman Hill – 12" × 24"

Here two American themes, very different in conception and execution are juxtaposed. As with the Dawlish paintings, one is a peaceful daytime scene with the powerful freight locomotive hauling its load up a steep mountain gradient, while the other is a small but powerful night scene.

Cuneo has frequently expressed his admiration for the 'Big Boys' and in his earlier representation of the massive locomotive, again at night, the engine occupied almost the entire canvas with the viewer almost feeling in danger of being crushed by its mighty weight. Here, the artist has chosen to stand back further from his subject and the 'Big Boy', while still immensely powerful, has himself to battle against the elements of the natural world – the lightning and the pouring rain. The two sources of illumination making a telling contrast – the jagged natural lightning and the powerful beam of the lamp shining forward, straight and true.

←On the Way to Harding, South Africa
1988, 20″ x 30″

Meeting of the Gauges, Port Shepstone, Natal →
1938, 20″ x 30″

One of the South African railway freight routes, a 2 foot narrow gauge line, runs from Port Shepstone in Natal through the mountains to Harding. Narrow gauge trains have always had a special appeal for Terence Cuneo and these two works recall his delight at actually being able to drive one of the Garratt locomotives during a trip to Natal in 1958.

'On the Way to Harding' shows the actual locomotive that the artist drove steaming towards us in the middle distance, while at right a sister locomotive prepares to leave after taking on water.

In 'Meeting of the Gauges', the narrow gauge blue Garratt occupies the foreground position, while to the left two larger broad gauge locomotives sit on their 3 foot 6 inch track. Cuneo has always enjoyed pottering around locomotive sheds and shunting yards, sketching the engines and those who work on them and this painting has the relaxed but busy feel of such works.

The photograph shows the artist in the cab of a Garratt locomotive in 1958. Because of the confined space, Cuneo always drove these machines with one leg outside the cab and, wearing shorts, one leg would be burning hot, while the other was cooled by the breeze.

149

The Marshalling Yards, Johannesburg – 1989, 18" x 24"
Here in his most recent South African painting, Cuneo tackles a
complex composition unlike his usually more informal South
African works. Choosing a highview point, he surveys the wide
sweep of the marshalling yards where steam engines wait
patiently for their departure. The foremost locomotive moves
gently forward and the swirling steam and smoke, which partly
obliterates the gantry running across the top of the painting, is
very effective in creating a painting full of light and movement.

Sunset on Camden Shed – 1988, 30″ x 40″

In the 'Sunset', Cuneo has returned to his beloved 'Black Five' stalwart of the LMS and perhaps the setting sky reflects the fact that this class of locomotive hauled the final scheduled steam passenger journeys in 1968. Here she is seen leaving the depot at Camden, her swirling steam and smoke echoing the mauve clouds in the pink sky.

A Southern Express – 1988, 30″ x 40″ →

Meanwhile, the Southern Railways 'Light Pacific' 'Port Line' class No. 35027 prepares to pick-up her train on the Bluebell Line for the journey ahead. The Southern Railway has not featured in Cuneo's work to such an extent as the other regions, perhaps because it lacks some of the romance of the Northern routes with their 'Race for the North' or his beloved GWR with its beautiful coastal scenery.

153

The Duchess of Hamilton – 1989, 30″ x 40″

Here this magnificent LMS 'Pacific' takes on coal whilst preparing for departure. Cuneo has chosen to portray her from a similar angle to his 1978 version, but from a different side. The change of setting, however, from a daytime scene of rural tranquillity to night-time in the marshalling yards, creates a completely different atmosphere. The fronts of two other locomotives are just discernible behind the 'Duchess' and echo her powerful boiler form, while deep red LMS livery set against the almost black sky enhances her regal air.

The Class 91 – 1988, 30″ x 40″

It is fitting to end this survey of Terence Cuneo's railway paintings with his two latest commissions for British Railways, over forty years after his career in this field first began. Both portray British Rail's new Class 91 locomotive.

The first painting vividly captures the sleek lines of British Rail's new standard bearer, and also provides a fascinating glimpse of the artist at work. As mentioned before, Cuneo is, like most artists, reluctant to allow his work to be viewed before completion. However, in this instance, he agreed to photographs being taken at various stages and we can trace his progress from the early laying in of the colour areas which took place in his studio, through his return to the location at Bounds Green to work up the colour and check the general accuracy of the representation, to the finished painting.

I have discussed elsewhere that one of the requirements of a great artist is to choose the most telling vantage point. Looking at the photograph of the Class 91 and the attendant shunter, it can be seen that a lesser artist might well have chosen a view that showed just the '91', or the two locomotives without the elaborate gantries and wires above. However, when we compare the half-finished with the finished picture, we can see that these details make the painting work. The verticals and horizontals of the gantry contrast effectively with the diagonals of the '91' and the placing of the small cart carrying lamps is quite masterly in providing a foreground stop which contains the painting. To analyse the painting in this way is not to suggest that this is how an artist thinks; indeed, with an artist of Cuneo's eye and experience it is purely instinctive. Rather it emphasizes that just sitting down and painting an accurate painting is not enough.

Intercity 225 – 1989, 38″ x 48″

No 91001 'Swallow' accelerates as she comes across the viaduct at Durham. The painting went to press before the name and number were finalized – it should show 91001 in black low down beneath the cab window and a nameplate in silver on black on the panel aft of the Intercity lettering.

Cuneo has earned his position as the greatest railway painter of this century through years of experience, through hundreds of hours of painstaking study often in difficult conditions, through a tremendous love and enthusiasm for his subject and through that extra factor of having been born with an artist's eye.

Glossary of Paintings

Index

Tailpiece.→
Fred. Cheddar, O.G.M. (Order of the
Golden Mousetrap), for 40 years
Station Master at Little Gnawing
in the Wold on the Royal Caerphilly
and Volehill Central Railway.

The Mouse in 'Evening Star' (page 75)
is sitting on the bottom rung
of the foreground telegraph pole.